Nayna and the Jeep

By

Faith Naber

Edited by Paul David Robinson

Copyright 1952, 1964, 2019

Illustrated by Holly Carton

All Illustrations © 2019, Holly Carton

Kindle Direct Publishing Edition

Nayna and the Jeep

By

Faith Naber

Edited by Paul David Robinson

Copyright 1952, 1964, 2019

Illustrated by Holly Carton

All Illustrations © 2019, Holly Carton

Kindle Direct Publishing Edition

ISBN-13: 978-1-944675-20-2

ISBN-10: 1-944675-20-5

Nayna and the Jeep

Dedication

This book is dedicated to the wonderful people of the Philippines. It is a true story about a five-year-old Filipino girl and her first ride in a jeep in 1952.

The author, Faith Naber, was a missionary in the Republic of the Philippines from 1950–1954 on behalf of the Board of Missions of the Evangelical United Brethren Church. During that time she was married to Mr. Robinson who is in this story.

After returning to the United States from the Philippines, Mr. Robinson was a pastor and an activist with La Raza Unida; and Faith Naber became a school librarian.

Far away is an island with many mountains. The mountains are so many, and so steep that in some places there is no road through them. Right in the middle of the mountains is a village. Right in the middle of the village is a little grass house.

The little grass house has a steep roof. The house stands on four round posts. Under the house there lives a pig, and seven brown chickens.

Inside the house lives a family: There is a mother and a father; Melly, a big sister who teaches; Ahding, a baby brother so dear and sweet; and Nayna, five years old.

Because Nayna is five, she goes to school, and Melly is her teacher.

Melly knows many things. She knows that the world is big, that some people have blue eyes and yellow hair, that some people have milk for breakfast, and that some people have cars to ride in.

She knows a song about a jeep, and she teaches all the children to sing it. Every time they sing it, they point to the picture of a jeep in Melly's book.

This is a silly song for Nayna to learn. Since there is no road in their village, the children in kindergarten have never seen a jeep! But the children love school and they love Melly and so they learn everything she teaches them.

The children worked and played and sang. They learned new things every day. They are sorry when the last day of school came. But it was a beautiful sunshiny day. And there is a party.

From far over the mountains came a visiting teacher. Everyone stared at him. He had light skin, and green eyes, and a long nose. The visiting teacher talked to Melly and the children went out to play. But they didn't play. They stood outside the school room and looked at the strange man. They knew about people with light skin.

When the children went in for the party, Melly said, "This is Mr. Robinson. He has come to our party and brought us some sugar for a surprise."

Melly had cooked a big pot of sweet potatoes. She put a little of Mr. Robinson's brown sugar on a piece of banana leaf for each child. The children dipped the potatoes in the sugar. It was a wonderful party!

When the party was over, Mr. Robinson said to Melly, "Will you teach summer school in a village far away, a village where there was no teacher this year at all?"

Melly said, "I will go. But Nayna must go with me to keep me company."

So Nayna got her extra dress and the towel which was her blanket and she put them in the box with Melly's things.

Melly carried the box on her head. Mr. Robinson carried his pack on his back. And Nayna skipped along behind. Up and down the mountain they went.

Finally they came to a river. To go across the river they must get into a basket. The basket is on a cable fastened way above the water. Someone pulls a rope and the basket crosses the river.

On the other side of the river is a road. At the end of the road was Mr. Robinson's jeep just waiting for him.
Nayna said, "Look, Melly, at the funny house."
Her sister said, "That is not a house."
"It is as big as a house," said Nayna.
"Well," her sister said, "it is a jeep."

"But," cried Nayna, "a jeep is this big!" And she showed with her fingers the size of the jeep in Melly's picture book.

"That," said Melly "is only the picture of a jeep. Remember we had a picture of a baby but Ahding is this tall. We had a picture of a banana but a banana is this long."

Nayna stood still a while to think. "Oh!" she said at last. "That was a picture of a jeep and this is a real jeep!"

Nayna smiled then, and walked up to the jeep. She walked all around it. She stopped in front and said, "Look! God gave it two eyes, just like mine." Nayna patted the jeep and said, "I like this jeep. It's pretty."

Melly put her box in the back of the jeep. Mr. Robinson put his pack there too. Then all three got into the jeep.

Mr. Robinson put in the key and stepped on the starter.

Nayna heard a terrible noise and started to scream. "It's a dragon! It's going to eat me up!" she yelled.

She started to jump out of the jeep but Melly caught her.

Mr. Robinson turned off the key. "Nayna," he said, "this is the voice of a jeep. If a jeep doesn't talk, it can't work."

"Oh," said Nayna.

"See, we are not afraid," said Melly.

"Oh," said Nayna.

Nayna sat still for a while to think. "I won't cry any more," she said at last.

And Mr. Robinson started the jeep again and away they went.

Nayna looked out of the jeep. She saw the trees going by. She thought and thought and watched a while longer. "Look," she said in wonder, "the trees are running away!"

Melly laughed.

Mr. Robinson smiled.

Nayna looked at the stones and the road. She looked at the river. She looked a long time at Mr. Robinson. Then she turned and whispered to her sister, "Mr. Robinson is strong to push such a big jeep."

Melly was going to explain this, but just then Mr. Robinson said, "Listen, Nayna, the jeep has another voice. This voice tells people to get out of the way. Since we are coming to a curve in the road, I must make the jeep talk. Then if someone is walking on the road on the other side of the curve, he will get out of the way. Don't cry now."

"I won't," promised Nayna.

"Beep, Beep," went the jeep.
This time Nayna laughed and laughed. "It said, 'Beep'! It said, 'Beep'!" laughed Nayna.
And then Nayna and Melly began to sing together:

♪♪ "Beep, beep, the small jeep is coming down the street;
Beep, beep, the small jeep is coming down the street.
Stop, look, and listen! Stop, look, and listen!
Beep, beep, the small jeep is coming down the street." ♪♪

The End

Faith Naber in the Philippines *circa 1952*

Faith Naber was born on September 27, 1920. She was the third child of Peter Gombert Naber and Mary Orrila Grise Naber. She graduated from high school in Chicago, attended ECI in Evanston, and then Otterbein College. She married Frank E. Robinson in 1943. They both graduated from Otterbein College in 1944. They were missionaries to the Philippines for the Board of Missions of the Evangelical United Brethren Church from 1950-1954. After returning from the Philippines, Frank was a pastor and an activist with La Raza Unida. Faith became a school librarian.

Frank E. Robinson and Faith Naber had five children. They were divorced in 1976. Faith Naber died on April 7, 2007 after a short illness.

During her lifetime, she was a wonderful story teller during children's hour at libraries and when she volunteered as a clown in children's wards at area hospitals. She wrote articles for various denominational publications and many short stories that were never published.

Nayna and the Jeep is a true story about a five-year-old Filipino girl and her first ride in a jeep in 1952. Faith would tell it to children everywhere she visited on behalf of the Board of Missions of the Evangelical United Brethren Church. It is illustrated by Holly Carton and edited by Paul David Robinson.

Dear Reader,

You can find TALLWEED, another book by Faith Naber which is also edited by her son, Paul David Robinson. Click here:

https://www.amazon.com/Tallweed-Faith-Naber/dp/154424486X

Faith Naber, our mother and grandmother, wanted to share with us what it was like to grow up in Mount Greenwood during the great depression. Mount Greenwood is a neighborhood on the southwest side of Chicago, Illinois.

She started her book, TALLWEED, at the beginning of her first memory of THE HOUSE that her parents built. They built it as they could afford it. They never had a mortgage.

Today, the authorities would not permit a family with four children to live in a wall tent on the floor of a house without walls or a roof through a Chicago winter. In 1924, that is what they did. Faith Naber was four-years-old at the time.

Paul David Robinson
March 6, 2017

Faith Naber (1920-2007) - *in her own words* —
educator, librarian

Faith Naber was American librarian, educator. Certified school librarian K-12, Illinois. Leader Buckeye Trails council Girl Scouts United States 1955-1956, Wapahani council, 1957-1962; member Commission on Status and Role of Women, Northern Illinois Conference United Methodist Church, 1978-1994. Member American Association of University Women (program chairman 1987-1994, legislation chair 1987-1991), Coalition Labor Union Women.

Background

Naber, Faith was born on September 27, 1920 in Miltonvale, Kansas, United States. Daughter of Peter Gombert Naber and Mary Orilla (Grise) Naber.

Education

Associate of Arts, Kendall College, 1942; AB, Otterbein College, 1944; Postgraduate, Hartford Seminary, Connecticut, 1950; Master of Library Science, Ball State University, 1970; Postgraduate, Chicago State University, 1983.

Career

Education missionary Methodist Church, Philippines, 1950-1955; Teacher Mississinewa Valley School, Union City, Ohio, 1957-1960; Librarian numerous secondary schools, 1962-1970, Bluffton (Ohio) Public Library, 1970-1971; H.H. Conrady Junior High School, Hickory Hills, Illinois, 1971-1986; Consultant Chicago State University, 1976-1980; Orchard Hill Farm School, Tinley Park, Illinois, since 1976.

Major achievements

Certified school librarian, K-12, Illinois.

Works

Author: Philippine Dialect Primers. Unpublished children's story: **Nayna and the Jeep.**

Membership

Leader Buckeye Trails Council Girl Scouts United States 1955-1956, Wapahani council, 1957-1962; Member Commission on Status and Role of Women, Northern Illinois Conference United Methodist Church, 1978-1994; Member American Association of University Women (program chairman 1987-1994, legislation chair 1987-1991); Coalition Labor Union Women.

Personality

Interests: Flowers, storytelling, world travel, children, and photography.

Connections

Married Frank E. Robinson, September 5, 1943 (divorced July 1976). Children: Paul David, Mary Martha Howard, John Timothy, Faith Ann Robinson-Renner, Frank Eric.

Dear Reader:

One of Faith Naber's seven grandchildren, Scott Andrew Robinson, wrote a book entitled **Solar Energy**. You might want to check it out. Scott has autism spectrum disorder.

https://www.amazon.com/dp/B014JVLQY4

Paul David Robinson

July 27, 2019

Books by Paul David Robinson for young readers:
When the Dew Fell on the Okra is a children's story about the first Christmas ever celebrated in the land and imps and elves. Thanks to Rebecca Swift, the illustrator, it is now available for you to give to someone you care about.

First Eighty-five Poems is an autobiography in poetry and tells how the author decided to become a minister. The six other books of poetry are for adults.

Our Call to Serve tells the philosophy of life that came out of that decision.

Before My Shotgun Wedding is a book for all ages. It is about two best friends growing up in the mountains of Kentucky in 1952 and going to college before an abusive father with a shotgun forces them to get married. The sequel, **After My Shotgun Wedding** is for adult readers.

Ruth's Adventure is about an eight-year-old girl and her adventures with her family and friends in Colorado in 1904.

Allie's Adventure on the Solar Wind is about the first baby girl to be born secretly on a spaceship traveling between Jupiter and Mars.

Meld School Runaway is about a girl who was born with the minds of two boys in her head. Later she learned how to get into the minds of anyone in the world and know what they were thinking.

LIGHT AND TENDER BLUE and other stories from the sixties is a collection of fourteen short stories or novelettes written between 1960 and 1964. One or more can be labelled: Science fiction, Fantasy, Horror, Romance, Race Relations, or Satire.

www.ingramcontent.com/pod-product-compliance
Lightning Source LLC
Chambersburg PA
CBHW041539040426
42446CB00002B/160